BLITZKRIEG
FRANCE
1940

BLITZKRIEG FRANCE 1940

MICHAEL OLIVE
ROBERT EDWARDS
Foreword by Chris Evans

STACKPOLE
BOOKS

Copyright © 2013 by Stackpole Books

Published in 2013
by STACKPOLE BOOKS
5067 Ritter Road
Mechanicsburg, PA 17055
www.stackpolebooks.com

Cover design by Caroline M. Stover

Printed in the United States of America

10 9 8 7 6 5 4 3 2 1

Library of Congress Cataloging-in-Publication Data

Olive, Michael.
    Blitzkrieg France 1940 / Michael Olive and Robert Edwards ; with a foreword by Chris Evans.
        p. cm. — (Stackpole military photo series)
    Includes bibliographical references.
    ISBN 978-0-8117-1124-1
    1. World War, 1939–1945—Campaigns—France. 2. Lightning war. I. Edwards, Robert. II. Title.
    D755.2.O55 2012
940.54'214—dc23   2012040023

CONTENTS

FOREWORD

In the course of six weeks in the summer of 1940 beginning on May 10, the armies of France, Belgium, and Holland as well as the British Expeditionary Force—sent to the continent to support their allies—were routed by the German *Wehrmacht* in a stunning display of the new, modern form of warfare known as *blitzkrieg*. That France would fall in less than two months of fighting was shocking, certainly when compared to the stalemate battle of attrition of the First World War, when France successfully held the Germans at bay for four bloody years. How, it is fair to ask, could a once mighty military—supported by allies—be defeated so quickly and resoundingly?

On paper, the French military was formidable in 1940. With 5,000,000 men under arms; the massive and technically state-of-the-art defensive wall—the Maginot Line—that stretched the length of France's border with Germany, in addition to elements of the line that extended all the way to the English Channel to the north and as far south as the Alps; and tanks like the thirty-ton Char B1, equipped with both a 75mm and 47mm gun and armor up to two and a quarter inches thick, France appeared capable of grinding down the German *blitzkrieg* and avoiding the fate suffered by Poland in September 1939.

Facing the French across the Maginot Line, the German *Wehrmacht* did not at first glance appear likely to race across France. Unlike the French and British, very little of the German Army was motorized, instead relying primarily on horses and rail to move troops, heavy weapons, and supplies. However, the *panzer* forces—

in conjunction with the *Luftwaffe*—would combine to punch through the Allies' lines again and again, fighting and maneuvering at a pace far more rapid than the French and British were able to cope with.

France would sign an armistice with Germany on June 22, 1940, a swift and humiliating defeat made all the more bitter by Adolf Hitler's insistence that the ceremony be held in the same rail car in which Germany had signed its surrender at the end of the First World War. How the German *Wehrmacht* was able to accomplish this remarkable feat of arms is the subject of many narratives, including several in the Stackpole Military History Series. What *Blitzkrieg France 1940* sets out to do is illustrate those ferocious six weeks of fighting with hundreds of photographs—many taken by the soldiers themselves—detailing the rapid German advance and the brave but ultimately doomed defense of the French and British forces arrayed against them, culminating in the epic withdrawal of the BEF and many French soldiers from the beaches of Dunkirk.

Once again, Second World War military history experts Michael Olive and Robert Edwards provide context and technical information for the vast array of photographs, including the eight-page color insert featuring uniforms and weapons. The battle and, ultimately, fall of France are lavishly illustrated, providing a substantial and vivid account of those six terrible weeks.

Chris Evans
Editor
Stackpole Books

INTRODUCTION

POLAND AND THE "PHONY WAR"

On the morning of September 1, 1939, German forces invaded Poland. On September 3, Britain and France declared war on Germany in accordance with their treaty obligations.

The supposedly powerful Polish Army was decisively defeated and the country overrun in a matter of weeks. The fall of Warsaw on September 28 effectively ended the campaign, although there were some minor engagements lasting into early October.

During this time, the Western Allies did virtually nothing to effectively come to the aid of the Poles.

There was a tentative advance by the French against the thinly held German border. The so-called "Saarland offensive" was launched on September 7 by nine French divisions. These forces penetrated a distance of five miles along a sixteen-mile front, occupying a handful of insignificant villages.

The troops then halted and there was no further advance although German opposition was almost nonexistent. When Polish resistance collapsed, the troops were pulled back, and by October 4, all forces had withdrawn to the French frontier. Not a single German soldier was diverted from the assault on Poland.

The rapid conquest of Poland shocked the Western Allies and revealed to the world the revolutionary *blitzkrieg* ("lightning war")

concept of independent, fast-moving armored formations penetrating far into the battlefield, in conjunction with devastating tactical air support, causing a fatal dislocation of opposing armies deep behind the front.

The period from September 3, 1939, to May 9, 1940, was known in the West as the "Phony War" as both the German and Allied armies sat behind their respective frontiers. The French and British continued constructing fortifications and planning for the counterstroke to the expected German offensive. The Germans started planning for the attack on Western Europe.

Hitler's territorial ambitions lay in the East, not the West, and the decision of the British and French governments to declare war was not expected, given their recent history of appeasement over German territorial gains. When Hitler's tentative peace feelers in early October 1939 were rejected, there was really no alternative than to launch an attack in the West.

FALL GELB AND _SICHELSCHNITT_

The first German war directive concerning the attack in the West was Directive Number 6 for the Conduct of the War, issued on October 9, 1939. This directive called for the attack to be carried out in the autumn as soon as all plans were finalized and military units brought up to readiness.

The German General Staff was quite pessimistic about the attack on the West; the memories of the carnage of the Great War were still pervasive. This tentativeness was evident in the original plan they put forward, called "Case Yellow" (*Fall Gelb*). "Case Yellow" was not, as has often been stated, a rehashing of the Schlieffen Plan of 1914. That plan called for a massive enveloping movement from northern Belgium, pivoting on the coast, passing south of Paris, and isolating and destroying the bulk of the French and British armies.

If "Case Yellow" was a variant of the Schlieffen Plan, it was a distinctly anemic one. Essentially, it consisted of an enveloping movement on Ghent in order to separate the British Expeditionary Force from the French forces, defeating both in detail. Air and sea bases were to be secured for later employment against England. This was fundamentally a frontal assault by both the *panzer* and infantry divisions. How the campaign would further continue to decisively defeat the Allies was not detailed.

The plan was later modified to shift the axis of attack south, but it was still basically a frontal attack with limited objectives. Hitler modified the plan with a proposed attack through the Ardennes to initiate a breakthrough at Sedan on the Meuse.

Unaware of Hitler's Ardennes variant, General Erich von Manstein, a brilliant strategist and Chief of Staff of General Gerd von Rundstedt's Army Group A, had developed his own plan for a major attack through the Ardennes. The Manstein Plan envisaged a decisive thrust through the Ardennes, across the Meuse, and to the English Channel, trapping and ultimately annihilating Allied forces north of the Somme. The plan was appropriately called *Sichelschnitt*—"Sickle Cut."

In November 1939, Manstein had consulted *panzer* expert General Heinz Gude-

rian on whether the *panzer* divisions could be moved through the supposedly tank-proof Ardennes. Guderian replied that it could be done but a maximum concentration of the armored forces would be necessary.

Manstein presented his plan a number of times to the General Staff, but the daring proposal was consistently rejected. In fact, Manstein's persistence became so irritating that he was removed from his position with Army Group A and sent to command an infantry corps far from the battlefront.

Just prior to taking command, Manstein, along with other corps commanders, met with Hitler on February 17, 1940. The forceful Manstein took this opportunity to present his plan to the *Führer*. Hitler was immediately impressed by *Sichelschnitt* as it contained his earlier suggestions for an attack through the Ardennes. The next day, Hitler presented the plan, claiming it to be his own, to Walther von Brauchitsch, Commander in Chief of the German Army, and General Franz Halder, Chief of the General Staff. Manstein did not receive any official credit for his daring and ultimately successful plan, which was finalized in all essential details by February 24.

Prior to this, the original plan was fatally compromised when a *Luftwaffe* light liaison aircraft was forced down at Mechelen just inside Belgium on January 10, 1940. The passengers were two army officers, one of whom was carrying a briefcase containing the detailed plans for "Case Yellow."

Although Hitler originally wanted the attack to proceed as soon as possible, the necessity for a new plan and a particularly harsh winter meant that the offensive was postponed until the spring. May 10 was the chosen date for "A (Attack) Day."

THE ALLIED PLANS

The Allied defense plans were based on the assumption that the Germans would launch their attack through northern Belgium and southern Holland as they had in the Great War. Three plans were considered based on defense lines along the Albert Canal, the River Dyle, and the River Escaut (Schelde). The Belgians naturally favored the "Albert Canal Plan" as it protected all of their country, but it was considered too risky by the French General Staff as it gave the Germans too much room to maneuver. The "Escaut Plan" was rejected for exactly the opposite reason—it would presuppose the surrender of Brussels and provided no possibility for a link with the Dutch defenses. The "Dyle Plan" was a not wholly satisfactory compromise, establishing a defensive front on the Dyle River in order to protect Brussels. Strong forces were also positioned along the vaunted Maginot Line.

As both Holland and Belgium were neutral, a move by Allied forces into Belgium could only be made if invited to do so by its government. This hampered the construction of permanent fortifications along the Dyle Line.

The "Dyle Plan" played directly into German hands. If, in response to a German northern offensive, the Allies moved the bulk of their first-line infantry and mobile divisions into Belgium, an unexpected and powerful offensive through the Ardennes—considered by the Allies to be impassable for armored vehicles—to the Channel coast would completely isolate those forces.

The balance of opposing forces on the Western Front in May 1940 was as follows:

French, British, Belgian, and Dutch forces: 3,644,000 troops in 143 divisions, 3,500 armored vehicles, 17,500 artillery and antiaircraft guns, and approximately 2,280 aircraft.

German forces: 2,400,000 troops in 136 divisions (including ten *panzer* divisions), 2,574 armored vehicles, 16,700 artillery and antiaircraft guns, and 2,750 aircraft. The Germans were superior only in numbers of aircraft but could still count on an overwhelming superiority at the point of the attack.

THE HAMMER FALLS: MAY 10, 1940

While the Norwegian campaign was still in its final stages, on Friday, May 10, at 0535 hours, *Fall Gelb* was launched in stunning fashion, with devastating attacks by the *Luftwaffe*, rapid movement of armored and mechanized forces, and the daring use of airborne troops to secure key objectives.

In the north was Army Group B, consisting of the 18th and 6th Armies with twenty-nine divisions, including three *panzer*. The 18th Army was tasked with the occupation of "Fortress Holland," and the 6th Army was to advance through northern Belgium to the west, encircling Antwerp and Liege. In an incredibly daring airborne assault, eighty-five gliderborne troops of Assault Detachment Granite captured Eben Emael, a formidable modern fortress with a garrison of 1,400. Eben Emael was the key to the defense of Belgium as it guarded Liege and was on the direct approach route of the 6th Army. Despite being unable to capture an intact bridge over the Meuse or the Albert Canal, the Germans soon ferried troops across the waterways and constructed expedient bridges. The Belgian Army fought tenaciously but could do little to impede the advance.

In response to the German invasion, the Allied armies began closing up to the Dyle Line with thirty-five first-class French divisions and all of the 160,000-man British Expeditionary Force (BEF) with its sixteen divisions, including the 1st Armored Division. This advance was exactly what the Germans had counted on as, south of Aachen and Liege, the *panzers* of Army Group A were advancing toward the Meuse, their presence unknown to the Allies. The 15th *Panzerkorps* of Kluge's 4th Army closed up to the Meuse between Dinant and Namur on the evening of May 12 at the junction of the French 2nd and 9th Armies. *Panzergruppe Kleist* of List's 12th Army had advanced through the "impassable" Ardennes, easily brushing aside the screening cavalry divisions. Three *panzerkorps*—Hoth's 25th (5th and 7th *Panzer* Divisions); Reinhardt's 41st (6th and 8th *Panzer* Divisions); and Guderian's 19th (1st, 2nd, and 10th *Panzer* Divisions), comprising some 2,400 tanks—were about to force a crossing of the Meuse. Once across the river, these *panzerkorps* were the spearhead of the drive to the coast and the isolation of the Allied forces in the north.

Erwin Rommel's 7th Panzer Division was the first to cross the Meuse. The crossing was fiercely contested, and characteristically, Rommel personally supervised the bridge-building operations while under heavy fire. On the evening of May 12, Guderian's corps reached the Meuse and crossed with heavy *Luftwaffe* tactical support at 1600 hours on the thirteenth.

Despite the stubborn resistance of the largely second-line troops guarding the crossings and all the Meuse bridges being destroyed in accordance with orders, four *panzer* divisions were across by the evening of the fourteenth and driving headlong for the coast. By the evening of the following day, the last line of defense was broken. The heroic efforts of Allied pilots who continually attacked the bridges despite the massive anti-aircraft defenses and marauding *Bf 109s* was to no avail, and their casualties were crippling.

At this critical juncture, there had been no effective counterattacks mounted, and the Battle of France had effectively been decided in the Germans' favor. The French supreme commander, General Maurice Gamelin, had established his headquarters at Vincennes with no wireless communications, being completely dependent on telephone landlines. As opposed to the quick reactions of the German commanders, the crucial decisions were either not made or fatally delayed. On May 15, French Prime Minister Paul Reynaud telephoned Winston Churchill, Britain's prime minister since May 10, and stated to the astonished Churchill: "We have been defeated. . . . We are beaten; we have lost the battle."[1]

The "Dyle Line" was breached by Bock's Army Group B on May 15, which was much quicker than anticipated by either the Allies or the Germans. The Allied divisions in the north started to fall back, but the fast-moving *panzer* divisions were already in their rear. At that point, the German high command almost sabotaged their own successful operation by ordering Kleist's *Panzergruppe* to halt and not cross the River Oise before the eighteenth. The reason was that the cautious higher commanders, including Rundstedt, and the General Staff were worried about the open flanks of the armored and motorized units and wanted the much slower infantry divisions to close up and protect those flanks.

Guderian ignored the order and continued to advance, earning a severe reprimand from Kleist and precipitating a minor crisis as Guderian asked to be relieved of his command. Rundstedt and General List intervened, and Guderian was not permitted to relinquish his command and was allowed to conduct a "reconnaissance in force" as long as his headquarters remained where it could be easily reached. Guderian continued the offensive with his three *panzer* divisions, driving headlong to the coast.

One of the few tank-versus-tank engagements of the campaign occurred on May 15

1. George Forty and John Duncan, *The Fall of France: Disaster in the West, 1939–1940* (Kent: The Nutshell Publishing Co. Ltd., 1990).

when the 5th and 7th Panzer Divisions caught the French 1st DCR[2] refueling. The excellent Char Bs with their heavy armor and armament were immobile, functioning only as static pillboxes. More than 100 tanks were destroyed almost immediately, and after a night retreat, fewer than 20 tanks remained operational. The 1st DCR was destroyed without being committed to battle.

Colonel Charles DeGaulle, commander of the 4th DCR, counterattacked at Montcarnet, at that time the headquarters of the 1st Panzer Division, on May 17. Although the town was crowded with supply vehicles and logistics elements with few armored vehicles, the Germans hastily organized an improvised defense. The counterattack was repulsed without much difficulty and the *panzers* continued their advance unhindered. In fact, the attack was considered so insignificant that it was not even mentioned in the 1st Panzer Division's daily war diary. After the war, as a result of DeGaulle's fame, the attack of the 4th DCR tended to assume an exaggerated significance.

On May 20, Guderian's hard-driving *panzers* reached the sea at Abbeville after advancing ninety kilometers (56 miles) in a single day. The bulk of the Allied first-line forces were now trapped in the north, caught between two German army groups.

One day earlier, General Gamelin was replaced by the seventy-three-year-old General Maxime Weygand, who had never commanded troops in battle. Weygand found himself in a dire situation on taking command. In ten days of fighting, the French had lost fifteen divisions. In the north, forty-five more were in danger of

being encircled and destroyed, and the gap in the front, between Valenciennes and Montmedy, was now 160 kilometers (100 miles). There were no effective reserves, and the ammunition stores were almost gone.

On the same day that Guderian's *panzers* reached the coast, the only really effective counterattack of the campaign was launched by the BEF at Arras. The counterattack was mounted by the 50th Infantry Division, the 151st Infantry Brigade, and the 1st Army Tank Brigade with its heavy Matilda MKs I and II. Initially, this counterattack against the flank of Rommel's 7th Panzer Division went well as the shells from the standard German antitank gun, the 3.7-cm *PAK 36*, bounced off the heavy armor of the Matildas. Numerous German tanks and guns were destroyed, and at one stage, Rommel took personal command of the artillery and antiaircraft units firing at the tanks over open sights. The situation was restored by the evening of the twenty-first, but this attack sowed the seeds of doubt in the minds not only of senior commanders like Rundstedt and Kleist, but also Hitler and the General Staff. There was serious concern about the seemingly overextended flanks of the *panzer* divisions.

The isolated Allied divisions in the north were retreating toward the Channel ports of Boulogne, Calais, and Dunkirk, their only possible exits from the German army groups that were rapidly closing in. Lord Gort, the commander of the BEF, knew that the Battle of France had been lost and his responsibility now was to save as many of his troops as possible. The BEF contained the majority of the professional soldiers in the British Army and their loss would be irreplaceable if Britain was to fight on alone. Boulogne and Calais were courageously defended, the former until May 25 and the latter until the evening of the twenty-sixth. A defensive perimeter was established around Dunkirk with orders that it was to be held at all costs.

---

2. DCR—*Division Cuirassee Rapid,* French armored division, of which only three were operational in May 1940. The division had around 200 modern tanks consisting of two battalions of light tanks (Hotchkiss H39/35) and two battalions of heavy tanks (Char B1 bis), a battalion of motorized infantry and a regiment of artillery. Most of the French armor (about 80 percent) was dispersed among the infantry divisions.

Guderian's *panzers* were also closing in on Dunkirk but were given the order to halt on the May 24; the destruction of Dunkirk was to be left to the *Luftwaffe*. The reason for the order was never given—was it concern for the vulnerable flanks and need for rest and maintenance of the *panzer* divisions, or was it Goering's boasting that his *Luftwaffe* could destroy the trapped Allied troops? Whatever the reason, the halt order saved the BEF and thousands of French troops. In the early evening of May 26, the halt order was rescinded, but by then, the defensive perimeter around Dunkirk was firmly established. On May 28, the gallant Belgians surrendered unconditionally, with British troops taking over their positions.

The epic evacuation from Dunkirk, Operation Dynamo is well known, with over 338,000 British and French troops rescued from May 29 to June 4, with courageous French soldiers providing the rearguard. Britain's army lived to fight again.

THE FINAL BATTLE FOR FRANCE

General Weygand attempted to organize a defense in depth behind the Somme and Aisne Rivers, utilizing strongpoints centered on towns and villages, with the gaps in between covered by artillery and mobile reserves. However, Weygand only had sixty-five divisions left, and seventeen of those were either part of the Maginot Line garrison or second-line reserve formations. Additionally, more than 140,000 British troops remained in France after Dunkirk and were being reinforced as Lord Gort attempted to establish a new BEF.

The Germans commenced their attack on June 5 with Army Group B, which included six *panzer* divisions, and soon broke through the French defenses. By June 9, Army Group B had reached the Seine River, smashing the defending forces, and at this time, Army Group A launched its powerful assault in the center. The spearhead of the assault was *Panzergruppe*

Guderian with four *panzer* divisions. Initially, this attack was held up by the stubborn defenders utilizing numerous armored counterattacks and heavy artillery fire. Close air support from the *Luftwaffe* soon destroyed the supporting artillery, and the *panzers* were free to create their usual havoc.

On June 15, the Germans marched into Paris, which had been declared an open city in order to save it from destruction, and the next day, the Rhone Valley had been reached. Reynaud resigned on June 16 and was replaced by Marshal Petain, the hero of the savage battles at Verdun in the Great War. Petain was under no illusions about the futility of continuing the struggle and asked for an armistice. Hitler's terms were delivered on June 20, accepted on the twenty-second, and took effect at 2100 hours on the twenty-fourth. The Battle of France was over in a scant six weeks at a cost of some 153,000 German soldiers killed, wounded, and missing—a small fraction of the casualties sustained in the Great War.

Crucial factors in the Allied defeat were the deficiencies of command, control, communications, and intelligence. At almost every level, Allied communications were defective. Decision making was ponderously slow and therefore ineffective. By the time counterattacks were organized, the German forces had moved on. In contrast, the Germans reacted swiftly to any setbacks and immediately seized opportunities to advance—they were masters of the war of movement.

For all the success of the brilliant German victory in the French campaign, it fostered Hitler's delusion of the invincibility of the *Wehrmacht* and the infallibility of his decision making, which would have disastrous consequences in subsequent campaigns.

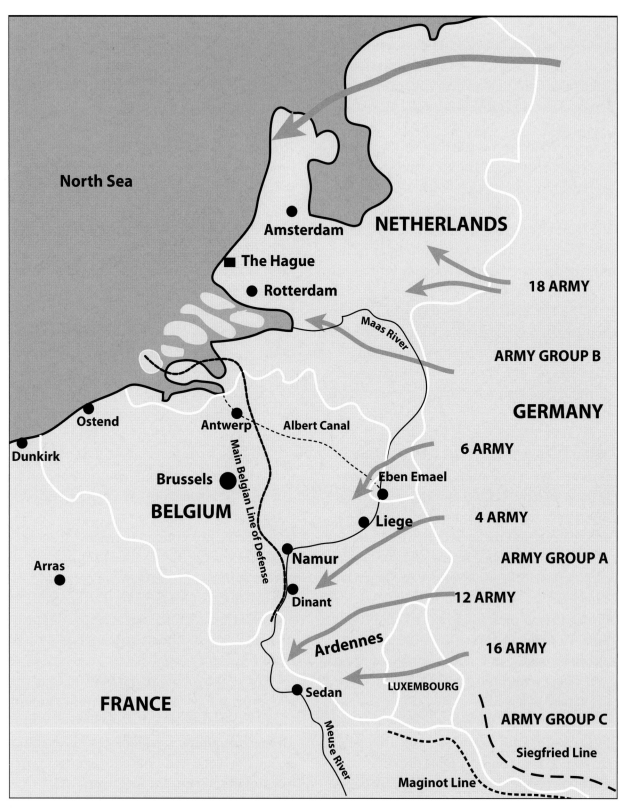

The final variant of "Case Yellow." Army Group B advances to the Dyle Line, causing the Allied armies to advance to the north. Army Group A is able to advance relatively unhindered through the Ardennes and reach the Meuse. From the Meuse, the *panzer* divisions break through to the coast.

THE INFANTRY

French *poilus* pose for a comrade outside a makeshift dugout. Given the overcoats and the barren trees, this image was probably taken during the winter of 1939–40 during the so-called "Phony War" that took place along the borders of France and Germany. In Germany, it was known as the *Sitzkrieg*—"Sitting War"—a play on words for *Blitzkrieg*.

The spoils of war . . . soldiers of the army and airmen of the *Luftwaffe* examine a French tri-color that has been captured. There must be something of interest on the flag, as evidenced by the *Unteroffizier* taking notes as the officer points.

A makeshift field grave for fallen French soldiers.

A *Luftwaffe* soldier poses in front of a bunker with his *MP 40* machine-pistol.

Field-expedient methods used to cross a canal, with commercial or private watercraft being used to span the obstacle and additional planking material added to reach either bank. Obviously, this was not intended for ferrying vehicles, but it did allow infantry to cross without getting wet.

In the absence of bridging assets or while waiting for the same, engineers sometimes constructed ferries capable of allowing vehicles to cross waterways This was obviously not the preferred method, since it was slow and cumbersome, but it was sometimes the only method available.

Here we see soldiers in front of a beached French vessel, probably a destroyer. This image may have been taken in the aftermath of the Dunkirk evacuation, when such images were a favorite subject.

Part of a machine-gun team moves out along a rural French road. Machine Gunner 1 carries an *MG 34*, the standard infantry machine gun of the time, while Number 2 appears to be carrying ammunition boxes. In contravention of orders regarding operational security, the men continue to wear shoulder straps with unit numerical designators plainly visible.

A rather elaborate dugout that might have been used for artillery or mortars, judging by its expansiveness. It was probably originally French, since the German forces would not have had time to construct a "finished" product like this while on the attack.

By contrast, a more traditional infantry-style dugout is seen here. This does not appear to be a fighting position, but rather sleeping "quarters" or a command-and-control bunker of some sort, since there are no obvious revetments or fields of fire from it. During the lull between the first part of the campaign and the second, German units may have had time to build structures such as these.

Soldiers, given the opportunity to rest, enjoy a meal in the field and listen to a commercial-type radio for the latest announcements and music.

Luftwaffe troops congregate around what apperars to be a range finder.

An interesting contrast between the "old" and the "new": a horse-drawn antiaircraft machine gun moves down a cobblestone French road as part of a horse-drawn column, while a motorized element takes a break.

A machine-gun section, with the *MG 34* set up in the "heavy" configuration. The superb, lightweight *MG 34* gave German infantry units considerable firepower and was far superior to anything the Allies could field.

These soldiers appear to be catching up on paperwork or writing home. Of interest is the effort to hide unit designators on shoulder straps. The noncommissioned officer on the left has simply removed his, while the soldier in the middle uses the prescribed "slides."

French railway cars are used to transport German motorized elements. Because of the speed of the advance, the railway system was captured largely undamaged.

Luftwaffe gunners pose around their weapon, a 3.7-centimeter automatic cannon. Although the immediate area around the gun is camouflaged, the position itself is in a relatively open area. This allowed the gun to freely traverse while engaging high-speed aerial targets and also to act as an inviting target from the air.

Whenever possible, German mechanized and motorized units moved by rail to save wear and tear on the vehicles.

Luftwaffe troops, probably part of an antiaircraft unit. Cooperation between the army and the *Luftwaffe* was exceptional and far more effective than that of the Allies. *Luftwaffe* liason units were permanently attached to the divisions as well as higher headquarters.

Unloading what looks to be a large tent, possibly for a headquarters unit. Accommodations for combat troops were far less elaborate.

In the wake of the decisive victory, German noncommissioned officers play "dress up" with captured French uniform items. Scenes such as this were relatively common early in the war for the German armed forces personnel, when victory seemed certain. As the fortunes of war shifted, souvenir hunting was less frequent for obvious reasons: when fighting for survival, there is no time for such luxuries and, perhaps more importantly, no one wishes to be captured with "souvenirs" from the other side, since it could mean an almost instant death sentence.

As was typical of the early stages of the war, the headgear of the fallen soldier was placed on the gravesite in addition to a cross. After the campaign, the soldiers were often disinterred from the field burial sites and reinterred in rather elaborate military cemeteries.

Divisional or corps engineers have constructed a traditional segmented sixteen-ton bridge. Unlike permanent civilian structures, the bridge was relatively fragile in nature and only allowed the crossing of spaced vehicles, usually moving at a walking pace and provided with a guide. This type of crossing could take hours for a large formation and required considerable planning to ensure the right assets were sequenced properly for a continuation of operations on the far side. This bridge site has become administrative in nature—that is, it does not appear that there is any imminent tactical danger to it and personnel wait to cross "in the open" and without concern for "bunching up."

This position appears to be some sort of fighting or outpost position, since it is well camouflaged but also has a field of view to the front. Given the fact that these are *Luftwaffe* airmen, as evidenced by the "gulls" on the rank collar tab of the one individual, it is probably for some sort of *Flak* element.

Members of an infantry section prepare to move out. One man carries a spare machine-gun barrel (tube slung over his back), while almost all of the men have affixed wire to their helmets to enable them to apply field camouflage in the form of foliage.

Once time and the tactical situation allowed it, engineers set about constructing more permanent structures. If the existing civilian structure was destroyed or damaged beyond immediate repair, a semi-fixed structure was often built next to it since the crossing points and features were generally known quantities. In this case, wooden planks have been built and the edges apparently reinforced with railway track. A horse-drawn supply column crosses the structure. It was probably part of the field trains of an infantry division, since almost all of its "mobile" assets were provided with literal "horsepower."

A well-armed infantry squad poses for an impromptu photograph.

A mounted infantryman with saddle horses, probably used for reconnaissance. Despite the publicity given to the *panzers*, the German Army was largely horse-drawn–up to 90 percent of infantry divisions, which, in May 1940, typically had 1,700 saddle horses, 3,600 draft horses, and a veterinary company to take care of them.

Assault crossings were generally done whenever the far shore was defended. These relied on floats or pneumatic craft, either motor-powered or paddled. Generally, these types of operations were done at night, given the extreme vulnerability of forces moving in the open across a waterway in slow-moving craft against a defended position. In this instance, the river has already been forced and assets—apparently two manhandled 3.7-centimeter antitank guns—are being transported to the far side.

A 7.92mm *MG 13* being used in the antiaircraft role as indicated by the mounting and the ring sight. This is a posed photograph–there is no indication of any ammunition feed! Usually, the *MG 13* used a 25-round box magazine or a 75-round saddle magazine. The *MG 13* was superseded by the much superior *MG 34* in 1936 and was mainly used by garrison units after that date.

Soldiers of an infantry element wait their turn to cross an expedient bridge.

Once the campaign was over, most of the forces not immediately designated for occupation duties were returned to Germany and their home stations by rail.

A soldier has written, *"Mir ist alles Schnuppe . . . ich fahre zu meiner Puppe"* ("I could care less . . . I'm going to see my gal"), on the Type 82 *Volkswagen.*

French prisoners wait along the side of a cobbled road while a German motorized column passes.

Long columns of French POWs, in this instance guarded by a mounted infantryman. The first-class French divisions were sent to Belgium to man the Dyle Position, leaving second-line fortress formations, inadequately trained and badly equipped, to guard the French lines in the supposedly "tank-proof" Ardennes. Although the French soldiers defended bravely, they were soon swept aside by the attacking Germans. Surrounded, with no orders or supplies reaching them, they had little choice but to surrender.

Some "exotic" French ordnance and weaponry is put on display for German soldiers. Some of the weapons look to be of World War I vintage and may have been culled from battlefields of that era. German soldier accounts of the fighting in France often relate how units passed by or through World War I battlefields, where relatives also fought and fell a generation previously. By 1940, none of the World War I battlefields had been totally swept for weapons and explosive ordnance, which still posed a danger to passers-by and visitors. In fact, injuries are still reported annually to this day from previously unexploded ordnance in France.

A memento of the fighting for the photo album. The Germans were proflific takers of photographs, even though it was officially forbidden to do so. Note that two of the soldiers are wearing the flashlight signalling device.

The Napoleonic maxim that "an army marches on its stomach" is still true to this day. The field kitchen is one of the most essential rear-echelon items.

An orders conference as an assault unit waits to cross a river. The Germans made numerous river crossings during the campaign, most of them under difficult conditions.

"Newly minted" soldiers ready for the front.

The chance to relax is taken whenever possible.

A very nice posed shot of a soldier on guard duty.

An *Sd.Kfz. 222* armored car is ferried across a river on a pontoon raft. The Germans were masters of improvisation and quickly adapted to changing circumstances.

Where bridges are not available, the tedious job of fording the river becomes necessary.

The *panzers* received the publicity and the glory, but a large proportion of the transport capacity of the German Army consisted of horse-drawn elements that were an essential part of the campaign.

This staff car has seen its share of combat, but it appears to still be operational, if somewhat disorganized.

A break from the strain of combat was always welcome, particularly listening to music or news from home, even if it was strictly censored and often rife with heavy-handed propaganda.

The Infantry   27

An image that seems emblematic of the campaign in the West as a whole: long columns of infantry march down dusty roads in one seemingly ceaseless march against an ever-withdrawing foe.

Once obstacles had been breached or bypassed, it was necessary to make the roadway trafficable again. Here soldiers fill in a surface next to a railway crossing.

The different modes of transport are obvious: bicycles, horse-drawn vehicles, and trucks.

Horse-drawn trains elements follow a column of infantry down a dusty rural road.

An individual fighting position that is posed to show a soldier aiming an *MP40* submachine gun. While on the offense, positions usually consisted of whatever was available in the process of tactical movement.

These soldiers are wearing what appear to be *M43*'s, which were issued later in the war, although, because of the angle, they might also be *Bergmützen*, which were worn at the time of the campaign in the West. In addition, one of the soldiers is wearing a *Jäger* patch on his right sleeve, so it is possible that this stems from the *Blitzkrieg* era.

A well-camouflaged assault unit waits for the order to attack.

A motorized column bivouacs for the night, with the vehicles surrounding the tents offering protection in case of attack.

An engineer footbridge that replaces an existing civilian structure in a small French town. Some equipment appears to be in the process of being manhandled across, followed by soldiers with bicycles and a four-legged friend.

An 8.8-centimeter *Flak* and prime mover are carefully escorted across an engineer bridge that consists of both pontoons and fixed spans.

German engineer units were well supplied with pneumatic boats for river crossings.

A cautious advance through the arches of a destroyed railway viaduct.

An observation/range-finding unit observes enemy movments. Those not immediately required for duty catch up on precious sleep.

Captured French medics seem at ease in posing with German soldiers. Once the war turned decidedly in the Germans' favor, many junior-grade French soldiers were only too happy to lay down their arms.

An older-model Maxim *MG 08* machine gun, generally issued to second-line and reserve units.

The tragedy of war: a dead French soldier. Most French units fought bravely but were overwhelmed by the speed of the German advance.

Enemy bunkers were occasionally encountered, especially along the Dyle Position that defended Brussels and the approach routes into northern France. One bunker seems to have covered an important approach route, since a great deal of effort was expended in placing it out of commission. The steel-reinforced concrete has received innumerable hits from guns of quite large caliber.

An opportunity to "liberate" some fresh milk. Rations were often supplemented by local supplies from the civilian populace. In France, the locals were usually quite willing to trade with the occupying troops.

The destruction of a French horse-drawn artillery element, although, unlike the Germans, most French and British artillery elements were actually motorized.

An army *Gefreiter* taps into a keg of liquid refreshment. It is interesting to note that stocks of French wine, champagne, and cognac were maintained by soldiers and officers during the rest of the war and often passed out in the field on the occasion of special events or individual accomplishments. Of interest in this image is the fact that the soldier has hidden the numerical designator on his shoulder strap (lighter-colored patch) in accordance with orders issued prior to the campaign and designed to heighten operational security. Images are frequently seen where soldiers did not cover up the numerals in this manner but simply turned their shoulder straps upside down for the duration of the campaign.

A road obstacle of doubtful utility—even if defended, it can be easily bypassed.

A dramatic photograph of a near miss from a large-caliber shell.

SS troops, as indicated by the camouflage smocks, which were issued only to *SS* troops at the time. They probably belong to the *SS-Division Verfügungstruppe*. The vehicle may be a French AMR 35 destroyed by a German 3.7cm *PaK 36*, and the impressive cathedral in the background may be the one at Rheims.

Captured French personal kits, rifles, transport, and artillery. When overrun by the *panzer* units, numerous French formations abandoned their equipment and faded away.

What appears to be a shattered refugee column. Fleeing civilians were often mixed in with retreating Allied soldiers and suffered accordingly from the bombing and strafing of the *Luftwaffe*.

An obstacle such as this one could generally only be declared a nuisance, unless it was defended and not easily bypassed. Whether this one was defended is unknown, but it could apparently be bypassed quite easily.

These "Spanish Riders" were probably quite effective initially as an obstacle, since they seem to be "anchored" to both sides and there was a clear field of fire covering them. By the time this image was taken, however, they were merely a nuisance that had to be avoided while moving down the road. Wire could also be an effective obstacle against both infantry and vehicles when properly emplaced and covered by fire.

An infantryman negotiates a wire obstacle during a training exercise. If this type of obstacle had been encountered in the field, it most likely would have been cut or trampled as opposed to being gingerly crossed, as seen here.

During the campaign in the West, the *SS* fielded three formations of brigade and division size, all of which would become some of the most famous fighting formations of the war: the *Leibstandarte SS-Adolf Hitler*, the *SS-Verfügungs-Division*; and the *SS-Totenkopf-Division (mot.)*. The *Leibstandarte* was essentially a reinforced brigade, with four infantry regiments, two artillery battalions, an antitank battalion, and a reconnaissance battalion, among other assets. The *SS-Verfügungs-Division*, which eventually became the *2. SS-Panzer-Division "Das Reich,"* had three infantry regiments, two artillery battalions, an antitank battalion, and a reconnaissance battalion, among other assets. Finally, *SS-Totenkopf-Division* had three infantry regiments, four artillery battalions, an antitank battalion, and a motorcycle infantry battalion. At this time, none of these formations had any organic tank components. Generally, the formations acquitted themselves well, although the army leadership was still highly skeptical of the utility of the separate formations. By the end of the war, more than 500,000 men were members of *Waffen-SS* formations.

Jubilant *SS* troops at the outskirts of a French village. They cannot be identified by formation, but they can be identified as *SS* since they do not wear the national emblem on their right breast.

A towed 3.7-centimeter *PaK 36* antitank gun and crew stop to observe something in the course of their duties.

Members of the *SS-Totenkopf-Division* pose in front of their truck on a rural road in France. They can be identified by the collar tab featuring the death's head—*Totenkopf*—on their right lapel. The *Totenkopf* was among the most controversial of the Waffen-SS formations since it routinely used personnel from concentration camps to man its field formations.

Dead *SS* soldiers. Most wear camouflage smocks, a hallmark of *SS* personnel until the latter stages of the war. The *SS* pioneered the use of field camouflage and came up with innumerable patterns used on a wide variety of uniforms. The influence of those efforts can still be seen today in the camouflage patterns used in the world's armies.

A field telephone truck in the process of laying cable. Field telephones were more cumbersome than radios but far more reliable and less likely for messages to be intercepted unless the cable was tapped directly. However, the wires were vulnerable to artillery fire and being run over by vehicles, paricularly tanks.

A light staff car, based on a civilian vehicle, camouflaged by a shelter quarter. The column is parked under the trees for some measure of protection from Allied aircraft, which were very active despite *Luftwaffe* air superiority.

A captured Allied staff car. The soldier on the right appears to be wearing British battledress. The German officer is examining the contents of the vehicle for anything of use to the intelligence section, such as maps or orders.

The horses are the passengers for once, being transported in a *Kfz. 72* medium cross-country truck.

It is not possible to determine if this truck was ambushed or merely involved in a road accident.

German troops inspect abandoned and destroyed French Renault R-35 tanks. These variants are armed with a short L/21 37-mm main gun. The R-35 was the main French infantry tank and, with a maximum armor of 40 mm, was considerably better armored than the Panzer I, II, or III.

The victorious troops pose for celebratory photographs. They do not seem to be to concerned about the ammunition of the burning R-35 tank catching fire and exploding.

A German 3.7-cm *PaK 36* anti-tank gun that looks to have been crushed, possibly by a French tank. The French S-35 and Char B heavy tanks had little to fear from the *PaK 36*.

Masses of German infantry pause before renewing the offensive—it was the infantryman's maxim to rest whenever he had the opportunity. The motorcycle is probably a 350-cc DKW.

A wounded *panzer* commander (as indicated by the throat microphone) and his crew.

The famous *Luftwaffe* ace Adolf Galland. During the Battle of France, he was a *Hauptmann* (captain) and later a *Major* with *1./JG 27*. His first victory during the battle was a British Hurricane.

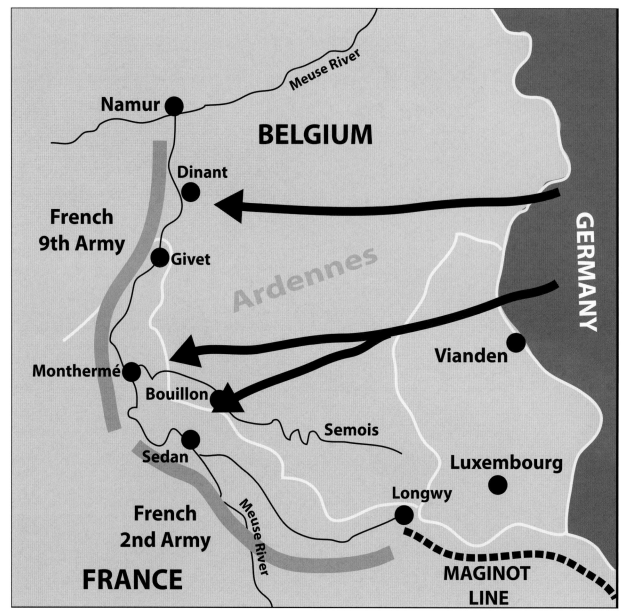

The *panzer* divisions brush aside all opposition in the Ardennes and advance to Dinant, Monthermé, and
Sedan in order to cross the Meuse and break into central France

A crew posing with its F model *Panzer III* (longer 5-centimeter main gun) around the time of the campaign or shortly thereafter, as evidenced by the wear of the field-gray overseas caps on the enlisted personnel, which were not replaced by black caps until later in 1940. In addition, the officer, recognizable by his visor cap, has both the Iron Cross, First Class, and the Armor Assault Badge—the *Panzerkampfabzeichen*—awards generally presented after the campaign was over and had not been presented in large numbers prior to the campaign. The *Panzer III* is instantly recognizable in profile by its suspension, which features six roadwheels with three return rollers. Like almost all German tank designs, the vehicle's drive sprockets were located in the front and the idler wheel in the rear.

A later-model *Panzer III* moving along a French country road. Most of the crew ride on the outside, due to the early summer heat. This vehicle mounts the 5-cm L/42 main gun. All the *Panzer III*'s in the French campaign were the 3.7-cm models.

An early-model *Panzer III Ausf. D* with the 3.7-cm main gun advances through a French town.

A captured French Renault utility tractor used as infantry transport.

Essential to the success of the *Panzerwaffe* was the widespread use of radio—both voice and Morse—for communicating rapidly and reacting quickly to ever-changing situations on the battlefield. To that end, a number of lightly armored radio vehicles were developed, of which the *Sd.Kfz. 263* was one of the more recognizable and heavier versions. It was employed in reconnaissance battalions and also in motorized signals battalions and higher command elements. A lighter version of the radio armored car was the *Sd.Kfz. 223*. The vehicle also featured a large frame antenna, which could be lowered when not in use. The vehicle was based on the light armored car of the time, the *Sd.Kfz. 222*, but the 2-centimeter cannon was removed.

Although the *Sturmgeschütz III* as seen in this image would go on to become the most widely produced assault gun of the German Army during the war, fewer than fifty were available for employment in France. There were all A and possibly B models featuring the same main gun as the standard *Panzer IV* of the time, a short-barreled 7.5-cm weapon of 24 calibers. In France, the assault guns were employed as separate batteries, generally consisting of three platoons of two guns each. One battery was attached to *Infanterie-Regiment (mot.) "Großdeutschland"* (*Sturmgeschütz-Batterie 640*), while four others were also employed in the campaign: 659, 660, 665, and 666. The batteries were quickly expanded to battalions after the campaign and formed the nucleus of the *Sturmartillerie*.

A large number of tanks built by the Czechoslovak Skoda firm were impressed into German service as the *Panzerkampfwagen 35(t)* and the *Panzerkampfwagen 38(t)*, with the latter being predominant. The German crews liked the *Panzer 38(t)*, since it was fast, maneuverable, and mechanically reliable. Although it only fielded a 3.7-centimeter main gun, that was more firepower available in either the *Panzer I* or *Panzer II*, which were the most numerous fighting vehicles in German armored regiments at the time. The downside of the vehicle was its riveted construction and relatively thin armor.

The diminutive size of these tanks—indeed the diminutive size of almost all light and medium tanks of the period—is readily evident in these two images of the *Panzer 38(t)*.

A *Panzer III Ausf. F* of the *1. Panzer-Division* halted among a miscellany of German vehicles and infantry, including a *Kfz. 70* personnel carrier at left rear and a *Kfz. 1* light personnel carrier at left.

Sd.Kfz. 223's at a higher headquarters as indicated by the line of staff cars.

An *Sd.Kfz. 223* with British prisoners.

Recognizing the need for additional combat power and antiarmor capability on the battlefield given the constant shortfall in production for fighting vehicles, the Germans started developing tank destroyers early on. The *4.7-cm PaK(t) (Sf) auf Panzerkampfwagen I ohne Turm,* more commonly known as the *Panzerjäger I* and seen here, was the first in a long line of field-expedient efforts and factory-production designs that were fielded during the course of the war. In all, more than 200 were produced, using the chassis of the obsolescent *Panzerkampfwagen I.* The antitank gun used was the Czech Skoda 4.7-cm antitank gun. Ostensibly, four antitank battalions were issued the tank destroyer and saw combat in France, although only *Panzerabwehr-Abteilung 521* saw combat in the campaign.

An *Sd.Kfz. 263* six-wheeled armored radio car. Good communications were essential to the *blitzkreig* concept.

Two views of the *schwerer Panzerspähwagen (Fu) Sd.Kfz. 232* six-wheeled armored radio car, issued to motorized signals units. It was the ability of the fast-moving *panzer* divisions to quickly report the results of reconnaissance and receive timely orders that continually caught Allied units off balance.

A *schwerer Panzerspähwagen (Fu) Sd.Kfz. 231* eight-wheeled armored car, issued to the heavy platoon of the armored car squadron of each motorized reconnaissance detachment.

A *Panzerfunkwagen Sd.Kfz. 263* eight-wheeled armored radio car, issued to the signals detachments of motorized and *panzer* divisions as well as corps and army headquarters. The juxtaposition of the intimidating vehicle and the elderly lady walking along the rubble-lined street is particularly poignant.

The Germans made extensive use of half-track vehicles, although supply never kept pace with demand. The vehicle on the left is the *3.7-cm Flak 36 auf Fahrgestell Zugkraftwagen 5t*. The vehicle on the right is an early-model *Sd.Kfz. 11*, the standard artillery tractor.

A very rare photograph of an *Sd.Kfz 8* artillery tractor converted to mount an *8.8-cm Flak 18*.

Faces of the *Panzertruppe*. The four formal portraits show enlisted tankers in uniforms generally worn at the time of the campaign in the West.

The **top left** image shows an *Unteroffizier* in the earliest pattern of the *panzer* jacket, which featured a smaller collar than its later counterparts. These were introduced in 1935 and officially replaced by the second-pattern jacket around 1937, although instances of wear of the first-pattern jacket can be seen all the way until the end of the war. These noncommissioned officers wear the combination beret and crash helmet that was issued from the onset of the tank arm in 1935 through the Battle of France but discontinued shortly thereafter, in part due to its unpopularity with tankers. It was replaced by soft caps, both the overseas variety (initially) and the billed field cap, the *M43*.

The **top right** photo shows the second-pattern jacket with its wider lapel and collars. The jacket continued to be piped in the branch-of-service color—rose pink for the *Panzertruppe*—although that would be phased out later in the war as a cost-cutting measure. Although the uniform was originally designed solely for wear for duty on or near the fighting vehicles, the basic design was so popular that soldiers started wearing it as a quasi walking-out dress uniform, as evidenced here by the wear of badges and the marksmanship lanyard for tankers, the *Schützenschnur*. This tanker was assigned to *Panzer-Regiment 23*, as evidenced by the numerals on his shoulder straps. The regiment was initially a separate formation with only one battalion that was not assigned to a division. It supported the *17. Infanterie-Division* in the campaign in Poland. By the time of the campaign in the West, the regiment had been assigned to the *7. Panzer-Division*, where it was redesignated as the *II./Panzer-Regiment 25*.

The **top** photographs on this page likewise show the wear of the second-pattern uniform jacket, with the soldier on the left being assigned to *Panzer-Regiment 33* of the *9. Panzer-Division.*

The image at **right** shows an unidentified tank regiment commander. As was typical with the pre- and early-war armor commanders, they had all seen service in the First World War, as evidenced in this case by the extensive medal bar he is wearing. This officer wears the first-pattern *panzer* jacket.

A riveted version of the *Sd.Kfz. 251 Ausf. C* armored personnal carrier. Generally, only one company of a rifle/*panzergrenadier* battalion was issued the half-track.

A heavily camouflaged *Sd.Kfz. 10.*

Designed as a training tank for the fledgling *Panzerwaffe*, the *Panzerkampfwagen I* saw combat service in the opening stages of World War II, including the campaign in the West, where it continued to be widely used. Featuring only two machine guns and a two-man crew, it was no match for most fighting vehicles employed by the Allied countries at the time, but it still gave a good account of itself if employed properly a well-trained crew.

In an early effort to provide more mobility for the artillery elements supporting motorized forces, the 15-cm *sIG 33 (Sf) auf Panzerkampfwagen I Ausführung B* was created. The *schweres Infanterie-Geschütz 33* was the standard heavy infantry gun in use by the heavy companies of infantry and rifle regiments at the start of the campaign in the West. In this configuration, it was mounted on the chassis of a *Panzer Ib*. Essentially a field-expedient solution to a vexing problem, the vehicle had both advantages and disadvantages. While it provided a degree of mobility heretofore not enjoyed by the gun and a limited amount of protection in an open-topped fighting compartment, the vehicle was top heavy and prone to mechanical malfunction, in addition to presenting a tall silhouette and not having a large amount of stowage space for ammunition.

A *Panzer I* and crew await transport on a trailer. It cannot be determined whether the vehicle is awaiting evacuation due to mechanical problems or whether is an earlier image of one of the tank battalions assigned to the light divisions in 1939 whose tanks were intended to be transported to the battlefield area on trailers and then offloaded in an effort to increase mobility and avoid wear and tear on the tracked vehicles. In any event, the light divisions proved to have significant tactical and organizational issues and were all converted to armored divisions prior to the start of the campaign in the West.

Two views of *Panzer II*'s in service with *Panzer-Regiment 7* (*10. Panzer-Division*), as noted by the bison insignia on the turrets. In the photograph below, the crew can be seen belting machine-gun ammunition together, since the rounds were delivered to the crews separately.

The *Panzerkampfwagen II* was the most numerous tank in frontline service by the German Army during the campaign in the West. It was on the verge of obsolescence then, but shortages of the *Panzer III* and the *Panzer IV* forced it to remain in the front lines as the mainstay of the *Panzerwaffe* for the period.

The gun mantlet of a *Panzer III* has been penetrated by an armor-piercing shell. The mantlet is only 30mm thick, so even a small-caliber round like this one could defeat the armor plating.

A column of *Panzer II*'s and *III*'s at rest before resuming the advance.

Motorcycle infantry and *Panzer I*'s pass an abandoned French *Panhard 178* armored car.

Liquid refreshment for the crew of a *Panzer II*. The name of a crewmember killed in action has been painted on the rear of the turret of the tank. This was relatively common practice early in the war, and it was also done in prewar years to denote comrades killed in training accidents. The crewmembers have also "misplaced" their beret/crash helmet combinations for a traditional French "Basque" cap, which features a national insignia and a "skull" from collar-tab insignia. This practice was also occasionally encountered—as long as it received the countenance of the chain of command—since the beret/crash helmet was almost universally disliked.

A completely burned-out *Panzerkampfwagen IV Ausführung D* is passed by a column of infantry somewhere in France. At the time of the fighting in the West, this was the heaviest operational tank in the German Army's inventory. It was intended primarily as a support vehicle, with the *Panzer III*'s conducting the tank-on-tank engagements, since its low-velocity 24-caliber-length 7.5-centimeter main gun was relatively useless against the armor of the day, particularly the heavy Allied tanks such as the Char B and Matilda.

In the foreground is a *Pz.Kpfw. 35(t)*. 219 of these tanks were confiscated from the Czech Army in March 1939. Seen in use with the *6th Panzer Division* in France, it was not as popular as the more numerous *Pz.Kpfw. 38(t)* shown below in a propaganda photograph on the English Channel.

An *Sd Kfz. 222* light armored car that has been hit by what appears to be an antitank shell. The *2.0-cm KwK 30* can be used against ground targets or aircraft. Issued to the armored car squadrons of the reconnaissance batallions.

An armored column on the move. The good French primary and secondary road network greatly aided the German advance. The roads would not prove to be so trafficable in Russia.

*Panzer III*s and *Panzer II*s, motorcycle/sidecar combinations, and *Sd.Kfz. 251* armored personnel carriers continue the relentless advance.

Sd.Kfz. 222 and Sd.Kfz. 232 (Funk) armored cars of *Panzergruppe Guderian.* German reconnaissance units had considerable combat capabilities and often led attacks.

A destroyed *Panzer II*. The thin armor is evident. In the background is a *Panzer I*. Neither of these vehicles was intended for combat, but a lack of tanks for the rapidly expanding number of *panzer* divisions necessitated their use.

Panzer I's lead this motorized column.

An orders conference between motorcycle reconnaissance troops and *panzer* crews. Effective reconnaissance and timely supply of information was essential to the maintaining of a rapid advance.

A totally destroyed *Panzer III*, possibly from an internal explosion of onboard ammunition.

A sixteen-ton pontoon bridge. German engineers constructed numerous bridges over the Meuse in order to facilitate the advance. Often, these bridges were constructed under heavy fire and were bombed continuously.

A heavily damaged *Sd.Kfz. 232 6-Rad/Panzerfunkwagen,* a six-wheeled armored radio vehicle based on the 6 x 4 truck chassis. One hundred and twenty-three were produced from 1932 to 1937 and issued to the reconnaissance detachments of armored and motorized divisions. It was armed with a 2cm *KwK 30* and a 7.92mm *MG 13.*

Relaxation and a chance to listen to some music for *panzer* crewmen. The vehicle is an *Sd.Kfz. 222* light armored car.

Track maintenance on a *Panzer IV Ausf. B* or *C*. The *Panzer IV* was Germany's heaviest tank at that time and was intended primarily for infantry support with its low-velocity 7.5-cm L/24 main gun.

FRENCH and BRITISH TANKS

This Hotchkiss 35 demonstrates the camouflage scheme to good effect on what appears to be an abandoned vehicle. Also clearly seen is the "playing card" method used to identify vehicles of a formation. In this case, the tank was probably assigned to the 1st Platoon of the 2nd Company of an unidentified element. In this system, the platoons were identified by the suits (1st Platoon = spades; 2nd = hearts; 3rd = diamonds; and 4th = clubs) and the companies by the sequence of the French national colors (1st Company = blue; 2nd = white; and 3rd = red). The location of these markers was apparently generally left up to the formation commander, with the sides of the turret and the hull rear being the most common locations.

Two views of a destroyed *Char 2C*. Its operational weight of sixty-nine tons made it heavier than any vehicle to see combat service in the initial stages of World War II. There were only ten of these vehicles in service, and they were used primarily for propaganda purposes, never seeing actual combat. After the first half of the campaign, the French decided to move the vehicles to the south of France to prevent their capture. While en route by train on specially constructed freight cars, their passage was blocked by a burning fuel train and the vehicles were destroyed to prevent capture. German propaganda later claimed that they had been destroyed by Stukas.

A Hotchkiss 35 light tank finished in the rather flamboyant French camouflage scheme of the period, which featured a hard edge and a variety of colors: *vert olive mat* (a matte olive green), *brun* (brown), *ocre jaune* (very light brown), and *vert* (light green). In addition, the French national roundels are on prominent display.

The small size of the Hotchkiss is apparent in these photographs.

The small size of the Hotchkiss is apparent in these photographs.

Another Hotchkiss 35.

The Renault *FT* saw wide service with the French Army at the start of the campaign in France. It featured a main gun in a rotating turret, the engine in the rear, and the driver in the front. Usually referred to as the *FT17*, more than 3,000 were accepted into French Army service over the course of its production, with some 500-plus tanks still in service among eight battalions and three separate companies, even though considered completely obsolescent by then. All were the machine-gun variant of the tank. After the fighting, the *Wehrmacht* impressed more than 1,700 of the vehicles into service for occupation duties and airfield defense.

More Renault *FT*'s.

German soldiers and airmen can be seen inspecting knocked-out or abandoned *Char B1*'s.

Abandoned *Char B1*'s and a Renault FT 17.

Knocked-out or abandoned Cruiser tanks (A13's) of the British Expeditionary Force, somewhere in France. The Cruiser had a suspension based on the Christie design and was fast and maneuverable (if underarmed with a 2-pounder main gun), but underarmored and mechanically unreliable. Some sixty-five were delivered to British forces, with most of them being lost in the battle for France.

A *Panhard 178* armored car under new ownership. The *Automitrailleuse de Découverte Panhard modèle 1935*, as the vehicle was officially known, was designed as a long-range reconnaissance vehicle. It fielded a 2.5-centimeter automatic cannon and a coaxial machine gun in a revolving turret, four-wheel-drive capability, a dual-driver system, and a range of approximately 300 kilometers. In all, some 491 were built for French service, with another 176 built after the armistice for German reconnaissance use. The armored cars used by the Germans were designated as the *Panzerspähwagen P204(f)*.

A Vickers Mark VI light tank, the standard British light tank at the beginning of the war.

A *Lorraine Tracteur Blinde 37L* tracked ammunition carrier. This chassis also formed the basis for several German self-propelled antitank and artillery pieces. Some 300 chassis were eventually converted.

The excellent French Panhard 178 medium armored car, equal or superior to any other armored car of its type in service at that time. The large wheels gave it very good cross-country capability. The Germans used captured vehicles in large numbers, with 190 available for Barbarossa in 1941. Its armament consisted of a 2.5cm cannon and a 7.5mm machine gun.

The Somua 35, officially known as the *Automitrailleuse de Combat modèle 1935 S (AMC 1935 S)*, was a French medium tank designed for employment with its cavalry divisions. It was a relatively well designed fighting vehicle for the time, with more than 400 being delivered to the French Army prior to the campaign in the West. It featured cast, sloping armor and a 4.7-centimeter main gun in a revolving turret and could reach a maximum road speed of 40 kilometers an hour. In tank-on-tank combat, the S35 could best the *Panzer III*, but it was hesitantly employed and often committed piecemeal. After the fighting ended in June, the Germans employed a number of the vehicles for training, occupation, antipartisan, and security duties as the *Panzerkampfwagen 35-S 739(f)*. BUNDESARCHIV, BILD 121-0412 / CC-BY-SA

A French medium Char D-2 tank. This was a twenty-ton vehicle mounting a 47-mm main gun, with maximum armor of 40 mm.

A captured Hotchkiss H-38. This was the French Army's cavalry tank. It had a 37mm main gun, maximum armor of 45 mm, and speed of 23 mph. More than 800 were in service in May 1940.

The
COLOR
of WAR

THE WEHRMACHT

Officer's M36
Field Tunic

Soldier's M36
Field Tunic

Standard Steel Helmet

M37 Feldmütze
Officer's Field Cap

Soldier's M34
Overseas Cap

Iron Cross, 2nd Class

Infantry Assault Badge

Wound Badge
Silver—3 Wounds

Soldier's Identity Disc

M1931 Bread Bag

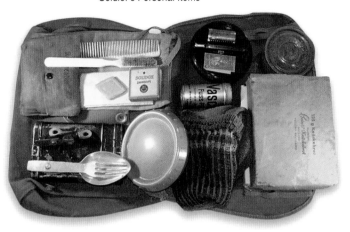

Soldier's Personal Items

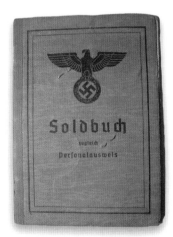

Soldier's Pay and
Record Book

M1931 Mess Kit

M35 Map/Dispatch Case

M1931 Canteen
and Cup

Leather
Marching Boots

THE WEHRMACHT

MG-34 Machine Gun with
7.92 x 57mm Ammunition Belt
and Case

Tellermine 35 Antitank Mine
with Carrying Case

Gear and Webbing Harness
Typically Worn by Infantry Soldiers

KAR98k Bolt-Action Rifle 7.92mm

Bayonet and Five-Round
Ammunition Clips

P08 Luger

P38 Walther 9mm

Walther 7.65mm PPK

MP40 with Magazine Pouch
and Luger Holster

KAR98k Ammunition Pouch

Entrenching
Tool

M1928 Stick Grenade

Gas Mask Canister

THE FRENCH ARMY

MAS Model 1936 7.5mm Bolt-Action Rifle

M1886 8mm Lebel Bolt-Action Rifle with Bayonet

Hotchkiss 8mm Heavy Machine Gun

FM 1924 M29 7.5mm Light Machine Gun

Infantry Soldier's Forage Cap

Artillery Corporal's Forage Cap in Bluish-Gray Wool

1936-Style Infantry Officer's Tunic

M26 Adrian Steel Helmet
(used by the artillery as evidenced by the crossed cannons on the front)

M1938 Infantry Soldier's Breeches

Composite Paper Leg Wraps

Gas Mask Carrying Bag

M1935 Mess Kit

Leather Cartridge Belt and Ammunition Pouches

THE BRITISH ARMY

Mark II Steel
Combat Helmet

Visor Cap Made of Olive Drab Wool
(badge is of The King's Royal Rifle Corps)

Overseas Cap Made of
Khaki-Colored Twill

Battledress Tunic for Lieutenant
Colonel of the Royal Engineers

Entrenching Tool
and P37 Pattern
Carrier

Mark V Gas Mask

P37 Pattern Bren
Gun Ammo Pouch

P37 Pattern Large Webbed
Canvas Haversack

Lee Enfield Mark 1 .303 Bolt-Action Rifle

Vickers Water-Cooled
.303 Machine Gun

Bren .303 Light
Machine Gun

THE PANZERTRUPPEN

Panzer "Wrap" for Officer
in Armored Reconnaissance

Collar Tabs worn
by Panzermen

M38 Officer's Field Cap

Panzer Crash Helmet
with Cloth Beret Covering

THE WAFFEN SS

Officer's Field Cap
(missing chin cord)

Officer's M40
Overseas Cap

Steel Helmet

Runic Collar Tab
Worn on Right Side
of SS Uniforms

M38 "Palm Pattern"
Camouflage Smock

M40 "Palm Pattern"
Camouflage Smock
with Army Splinter
Camouflage Repairs

An excellent photograph of the formidable Char B-1 medium tank, which had one 75-mm gun, one 47-mm gun, and a 7.5-mm machine gun. Its maximum armor of 60 mm was generally impervious to the standard 3.7-cm main tank gun of the *Panzer III* and the *PaK 36*, the standard German antitank gun. A serious limitation was the one-man turret, but the Char B was superior to all German tanks then in service.

A knocked-out Renault UE/AMX armored supply vehicle.

Another very good shot of an abandoned Char B-1. These vehicles were technically complex, and more were put out of action because of mechanical failure than were destroyed in combat.

Renault FT-17/18s. These tanks were relics from World War I. They were thinly armored and mounted only a machine gun.

A captured Char B-1 being inspected. The 223rd *Panzer* Company took four B-2 variants to Russia in 1941, and seven were used in the Balkans by *7. SS-Division Prinz Eugen* for antipartisan duties.

Another view of a Char B-1.

Captured Renault R-35s. The two in the rear feature a multicolor camouflage scheme of dark green and two shades of brown and light green.

A Char B-1.

The remains of a Panhard P-178 medium armored car mounting a 25-mm automatic cannon. This excellent vehicle was the most technically advanced armored car of the French forces in May 1940, with 360 in service. Captured vehicles were used extensively by the Germans.

French crewman are buried next to their destroyed vehicles.

A British Vickers Mark VI, standard light tank of the British Army. It was comparable in many ways to the *Panzer I*.

An abandoned Panhard P-178 armored car.

Somua S-35, the best French medium tank in 1940 and considered by the Germans to be the best tank they faced during the Battle of France, despite the limitations of the one-man turret. It was twenty tons in weight, with a very good 47mm main gun and 56 mm of armor.

Another view of the S-35.

A very nice photograph of *Wehrmacht* officers posing next to a captured Renault R-35. Note the rubberized overcoat of the motorcyclist, a piece of clothing particular to these troops.

A dramatic shot of three knocked-out Renault R-35s.

The FCM Char-2C super-heavy tank, which had a 75-mm main gun. Only ten of this sixty-nine-ton tank were built soon after World War I. The tank did not see operational service during the Battle of France as the railway track on which they were being transported from the front was blocked and the tanks were blown up to avoid capture intact. The one intact example was captured by the Germans.

Abandoned due to mechanical difficulties is this French Schneider AMC P16 M29 half-track. Approximately 100 were produced from 1928 to 1931, with about 50 available for service in May 1940. It weighed 6.8 tons, with an armament of a 3.7cm SA-18 cannon and a 1 x 8mm machine gun, a maximum speed of 30 mph (50 kph), and a range of 150 miles (250 kilometers). Because of the age of these vehicles, breakdowns were common.

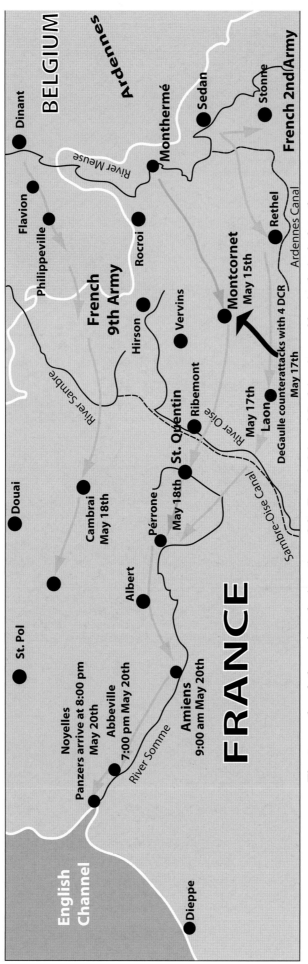

The *panzers* break through at the junction of the French 9th and 2nd Armies and begin their dash to the coast. DeGaulle's counterattack on May 17 and that of the BEF on May 21 achieved nothing.

A 15-cm *sFH 18*, the standard *Wehrmacht* heavy field howitzer. It fired a 96-pound shell to a maximum range of 12,600 yards.

A *Canon de 75 modèle 1897*, which was still in use in wide numbers in the French Army—more than 4,500 on inventory, according to some sources—despite its admitted obsolescence. The venerable "French 75" is widely considered by many historians to be one of the first "modern" artillery piece.

French static coastal artillery destroyed by the *Luftwaffe*.

A *Mortier se 220 mle 1916 Schneider*, a World War I–vintage piece still in limited service.

Another gun of World War I vintage still in widespread use by the French artillery was the *Canon de 155 Grande Puissance Filloux (GPF) mle. 1917*.

More abandoned French artillery. Many of these guns would see service in the *Wehrmacht* as part of the Atlantic Wall or as far away as the Eastern Front in 1941.

The breech mechanism for a super-heavy artillery piece, abandoned on its travelling cradle. Possibly from a *Canon de 240 L mle 84/17 St. Chamond.*

A *Panzer III Ausf. F*, possibly of the *8. Panzer-Division*. All *Panzer IIIs* used in the French campaign still mounted the barely adequate 3.7cm main gun. Although it has some track guard damage, this tank does not look disabled. In the foreground is the standard French light antitank gun, the 2.5cm *Cannon léger de 25 antichar SA-L mle 1934*. Due to its short range and the light weight of the projectile, this weapon was not very effective.

The speed of the *panzers'* advance often led to the capture of complete trainloads of weapons, such as these French medium artillery pieces probably of 10.5-cm caliber.

More 75's and *181/183 Canon de 47 antichar SA mle 1937/39* 4.7-cm antitank guns. These guns were capable of knocking out all German tanks then in service.

Abandoned modern French medium field guns. Although the French had substantial numbers of artillery pieces, many of them were from World War I and, although serviceable, were no match for more modern weapons.

Another abandoned French gun.

The standard German antitank gun, the 3.7-cm *PaK 36*, effective only against light tanks such as the Vickers and FT 17 and totally incapable of penetrating the armor of the French S35 and Char B or the British Matilda. It was soon replaced with the much more effective 5.0-cm *PaK 38*. The crew steadies the trails for firing.

One of the pre-eminent heavy guns used by separate heavy artillery batteries and battalions was the 21cm *Mörser 18*. This howitzer—*Mörser* is the German term for heavy howitzer—fired 21-centimeter separately loaded cased ammunition weighing in at 250 pounds a distance of 14,500 meters. The gun featured an interesting dual-recoil system, with both the barrel and the top carriage recoiling, allowing for a very stable firing platform. In the course of the war, more than 700 units were produced.

Using scissor binoculars to observe enemy positions.

The crews of a *10.5-cm leichte Feldhaubitze 18*, the standard German field howitzer. It fired a 14.8-kg (32.6-lb) shell to a maximum range of 10,675 meters. Although somewhat outclassed by Allied equivalents, this effective fieldpiece was in service until the end of the war.

A *10.5 cm leichte Feldhaubitze 18* battery in action. Even though the guns are camouflaged, the muzzle flash is obvious.

Two-piece rounds for the *15-cm schwere Feldhaubitze 18*.

The *15-cm schwere Feldhaubitze 18* was an improved version of a World War I design, the *schwere Feldhaubitze 13*, and saw service throughout World War II. Its 96-pound separately loaded cased ammunition could be delivered up to 13,250 meters at a sustained rate of fire of four rounds a minute. Some 5,400 howitzers of this type were produced before the end of hostilities, and the gun, although eventually considered outclassed by many Allied pieces, held its own during the campaign in the West and also has the distinction of being the first artillery piece to fire a shell with a rocket-assisted propellant (to increase range).

Camouflage netting to break up the outline of the howitzer, particularly from the air.

Rapid deployment of a *15-cm schwere Feldhaubitze 18* in an open field without camouflage. German artillery units often located their guns very close to the battlefield in order to give timely and effective fire support.

More images of the *15-cm sFH 18* howitzer.

A *15-cm sFH 18* howitzer in the process of being limbered for transport.

The full crew of a *15-cm sFH 18* howitzer. This photograph was probably taken at a training area as the inscription on the shell indicates.

A *15-cm sFH 18* howitzer battery.

This gun experienced a burst barrel, most likely as a result of premature ignition of the propellant charge or a fault with the explosive shell itself. The barrel has been blown apart. This type of accident is sometimes more dangerous to an artilleryman than enemy counterbattery fire.

A line-up of s*chwere 10-cm Kanone 18* and *15-cm sFH 18*. It is evident how similar in appearance thes two field pieces are. The *10-cm K18* is distinguished by its longer barrel.

The *schwere 10-cm Kanone 18*. This was a large weapon in relation to its caliber, but it did have a high muzzle velocity, making it an excellent tank killer when firing over open sights.

The *schwere 10-cm Kanone 18* fired a 15-kg shell to a maximum of 19,075 meters (21,000 yards). The army considered the performance of this gun marginal for its size, but it was kept in service until the end of the war since no better alternative presented itself.

Spectacular photographs of an 8.8-cm *Flak* battery firing at night.

The prodigious ammunition consumption is obvious in this image.

Due to the high rate of fire, loaders had to be both very skilled and strong. The one-piece round is clearly shown here.

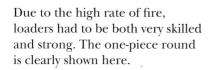

Arguably the most famous artillery piece of the war was the 8.8-cm Flak, which was fielded in a variety of production models, starting with the Model 18 in prototype stage in 1928 and progressing through the Model 36 (two-piece barrel) and the Model 37 (modernized). In addition, there was a Model 41, which was employed almost exclusively in homeland defense. All of the guns featured a caliber length of 56 calibers, firing a one-piece shell of 16.3 pounds. In the antiaircraft role, it had a sustained rate of fire of between fifteen and twenty rounds a minute. The gun was first used in a ground role in France, when standard German tank main guns and antitank guns of the day could not penetrate the frontal armor of heavy French tanks.

This appears to be a demonstration firing.

A third shot of the demonstration.

The four-meter Range Finder Model Em 4m R40 is the standard instrument for use with heavy antiaircraft guns.

The "88" was a true multi-purpose weapon: antiaircraft, antitank, and field artillery. In the diect-fire role, it was very effective at destroying fortified positions and bunkers by firing directly into the embrasures—a terrifying experience for the occupants.

Despite its formidable reputation, the *8.8-cm Flak* was a large target and, if not dug in, was extremely susceptible to ground fire.

The *8.8-cm Flak* was usually towed by the *Sd.Kfz. 7* half track. However, in this instance, a heavy truck is being used.

Elevation quadrant and elevating mechanism.

Setting the fuses—probably taken during a training excercise.

Field repairs being undertaken on this "88." Although these were complex weapons, the workshop personnel were very well trained and capable of repairing all but the most serious damage.

A destroyed 8.8-cm *Flak 18* with its *Sd.Kfz. 7* towing vehicle. The *Flak 18* weighed seven tons in travelling order. The half-track carried the gun crew of eleven men. Photographs such as this one, showing destroyed equipment, were strictly forbidden as they were considered to be bad for morale. However, this directive was largely ignored.

The standard light antiaircraft gun of the German Armed Forces, the *2-cm FlaK 30/38*, here in a semi-fixed position, probably in Germany. It had a feed system using ammunition boxes with twenty rounds and could fire at a sustained rate of 120–180 rounds a minute in the hands of a good gunner and crew. The effective ceiling was 1,645 meters (5,400 feet).

The *Luftwaffe Flak* units took a fearful toll of Allied ground-attack aircraft as they sought to destroy bridges and interdict the *panzer* columns.

Training on a captured 40mm Bofors antiaircraft gun. This was an excellent weapon and widely used by both Allied and Axis forces.

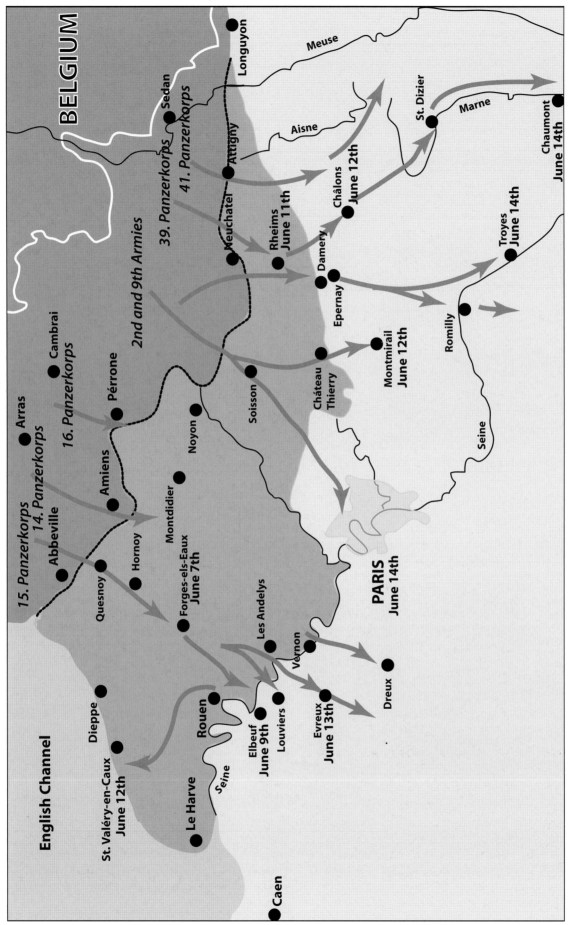

The final German offensive against southern France begins. After initial heavy going against Weygand's "Checkerboard" defense, particularly in the center, the *Luftwaffe* soon destroyed the supporting French artillery, and resistance started to disintegrate, with the remaining French armies trapped against the Maginot Line. British troops remaining in France were again forced to evacuate to England.

AIRCRAFT

Bf 109E's of *8./JG 54* at Guines airfield, France, in 1940. The *109* was superior to all contemporary Allied fighters, although the Hawker Hurricane and the *Dewoitne D520* could hold their own. However, *Luftwaffe* fighter pilots were in for an unpleasant surprise when they met the Supermarine Spitfire over Dunkirk.

A damaged *109* that would be returned to Germany for both repair and updating to the latest configuration.

Two views of the *Fieseler Fi 156 Storch* (Stork), a highly effective short takeoff and landing liaison aircraft. It was routinely used by division commanders to check on the progress of their units and conduct personal reconnaissance of the battlefield.

A *Luftwaffe* crewman rests on the tail unit of his *Dornier Do 17Z*. The Do *17*Z had a maximum bombload of 1,000 kilograms (2,200 pounds) and a top speed of 400 kilometers per hour (250 mph).

The reliable *Junkers Ju 52* tri-motor transport was also used to carry paratroops.

The terror of the skies over France in May and June 1940 was the *Junkers Ju 87B Stuka*. When operating where the *Luftwaffe* had established air superiority, the *Stuka* was a highly effective ground-support aircaft with the ability to deliver its bombload with incredible accuracy. The myth of the *Stuka* menace was born. The reality was that the *Ju 87* was obsolescent before the war started, being both slow and very vulnerable to fighters, as became painfully evident during the Battle of Britain. However, the *Ju 87* remained in service until the last days of the war. The *Ju 87* carried a 600-kg (1,100-lb) bombload at a maximum speed of 390 kph (238 mph).

An impressive line-up of *Ju 87 Stukas* on a large grass airfield. The lack of dispersement and camouflage suggests that hostilities have ended.

Deception! Dummy *Ju 87 Stukas* offer inviting targets to Allied pilots. Undoubtedly, there are numerous *Flak* units waiting for their unsuspecting prey.

The very oddly designed *Bruguet 274* reconnaissance/bomber aircraft. Maximum speed was only 236 kph (147 mph) and the bombload 120 kg (264 lb).

A *Bloch MB 152* fighter, with a maximum speed of 509 kph (316 mph), 2 x 20mm cannon, and 2 x 7.5mm machine gun. A rugged aircraft but inferior to the *Bf 109E* in all respects.

A *Mureau 115/117* reconnaissance/light bomber aircraft. The service ceiling was an impressive 10,000 meters (32,800 feet). It had a maximum speed of 340 kph (210 mph), a bombload of 200 kg (440 lb), armament of 2x 20mm cannon, and 4 x 7.5mm machine guns.

A *Dewoitine D520* fighter, the French Air Force's most modern fighter. It had top speed of 486 kph (303 mph), armament of 1x 20mm cannon, and 4 x 7.5mm machine guns. Only about seventy of these aircraft were accepted for service before hostilities began. The *520* was considered quite difficult to fly and was not the equal of the *109*.

Destroyed French aircraft, the fighter in the foreground is a Bloch MB 150. In the background is what appears to be an LeO 45 twin-engine medium bomber.

Despite the intense air battles between reconnaissance aircraft and their fighter escorts during the eight months of the "Phony War," many Allied aircraft were still caught on the ground when the *Luftwaffe* attacked on May 10.

An obsolescent Amiot 143 bomber. Top speed was around 200 mph, and its bombload was 3,500 pounds. The Amiot was easy prey for the marauding *Bf 109Es*.

A French Potez 637 reconnaissance aircraft, victim of a strafing attack.

A Loire Nieuport LN 401/LN 411 dive-bomber. Sixty-eight were produced for the French Navy. It was armed with two 7.9mm machine guns and a 20mm cannon and carried 500 pounds of bombs. Its top speed was 236 mph, with a range of 745 miles. On May 19, twenty LN 401s attacked German armored columns; ten were shot down and seven damaged beyond repair. All these losses were caused by *Flak*.

The excellent Messerschmitt *Bf 109E (Emil)*, superior to all other fighter aircraft during the battle, including the Hawker Hurricane. The *109* finally met its match in the Supermarine Spitfire over the Dunkirk beaches. This example is from *III./JG 77*.

A LARGE-SCALE BRIDGING OPERATION

The following series of excellent photographs depict an extraordinary bridging operation undertaken by German Army engineers. An extensive railway bridge is construced across a wide river valley. Barges are used to anchor wooden pylons in the river bed to support the massive timber trestles. A heavy railway crane is used to place the huge steel girders and lay the railroad tracks. A most impressive feat of engineering.

The pylons must be hammered deep into the river bed to provide support for the trestles.

A good detail shot of the intricate timber construction of one of the trestles.

The first freight cars are brought across.

Almost complete, the bridge can now support two locomotives. The bridge is now capable of carrying heavy military loads. Note the pneumatic boat tethered to the lefthand trestle.

A fine panorama of the finished structure. The length of the bridge is very impressive.

The long colums of French prisoners. The number of prisoners taken is not indicative of poor fighting qualities of the French soldiers. At Sedan, many second-line divisions faced first-class German assault troops supported by masses of artillery and overwhelming air support. The speed of the *panzers'* advance took everyone by surprise, even the Germans themselves.

A single guard for so many prisoners. Most French soldiers realized the futility of continuing to fight and just wanted to return home. Unfortunately, many did not do so until 1945 as the Germans continued to imprison French POWs until the last months of the war, when they were finally liberated.

The Germans attempted to exploit these French colonial troops for propaganda purposes. It would be interesting to know what these soldiers thought about fighting for a colonial power so far from their home.

British prisoners march into captivity, displaying good discipline and morale.

A column of *Pz.Kpfw. 35(t)* passes a group of French prisoners.

After the fall of France, many German soldiers were granted leave and explored the normal tourist sights and sounds of Paris and Versailles, as this sampling of images attests. It should be noted that both of those locations later served as schoolhouses for the ever-expanding German military, and both armor-related and command courses were taught at Versailles.

The most prized occupation posting was to Paris, where, initally, life's luxuries were easy to find and the Resistance Movement had yet to make its presence felt.

A *Kfz. 70* personnel carrier parked opposite a memorial to those French soldiers of the Great War that made the ultimate sacrifice.

No visit to Paris would be complete without a visit to the iconic Eiffel Tower.

One of the massive Maginot Line casemates—these were virtually impervious to artillery shells and bombs.

These steel observation cupolas were susceptible to direct fire from the 8.8 cm *Flak*.

This appears to be some form of roadblock.

A Maginot Line *ouvrage*. Much has been written about the folly of building these fortifications. However, the Maginot Line proper was never breached by the Germans, just the lighter defenses on the periphery of the line. The large fortresses held out until after the surrender, with some determined German assaults bloodily repulsed. The main problem is that fixed fortifications can usually be outflanked; if the French had sufficient mobile and armored forces to cover the open flanks, the German invasion might have gone very differently.

Luftwaffe officers inspect the extensive bomb damage. Generally, the *Luftwaffe* operated in a tactical role in the campaign and attacked strictly military targets. However, those towns where enemy troops were defending were legitimate targets.

Heavy damage to a French town—whether from heavy artillery or bombing, it is not possible to make a definitive conclusion.

Despite the devastation and chaos of war, life goes on. Crops still need to be planted and harvested.

A Maginot Line bunker with evidence of artillery damage.

Another view of what could be a pristine-looking Maginot Line bunker, although the construction seems German and the uniforms look prewar or very early war.

A bunker surrounded by barbed-wire entanglements and an ominous looking electric fence.

Numerous artillery hits around and directly on an artillery embrasure. The cannon looks to be a 75mm Mle 1897, the famous French "Seventy-Five."

Surrendering French tank crew.

British prisoners of war. The British troops fought doggedly against the fast-moving Germans, but like their French counterparts, they were usually caught by the speed and tactical flexibility of the German advance.

British prisoners.

Stacks of small arms and other equipment. During the latter stages of the campaign, demoralized French troops surrendered *en masse*.

Long columns of French prisoners passing a vehicle from the 5. *Panzer-Division*.

"Under New Management": the first signs of the German occupation.

The French Army had a number of divisions composed of soldiers from the French African colonies. These colonial divisions fought as courageously as the circumstances allowed. The Nazi propaganda machine was quick to exploit these troops for racial vilification.

More stacks of discarded rifles and light machine guns. The discussion between the civilian and the German officer seems quite animated. Relations between the French populace and the occupying German troops were reasonably cordial in the early days of the occupation.

German soldiers examine a captured Mitrailleuse "Hotchkiss" mle 8mm machine gun. This weapon was the standard French heavy machine gun in World War I and was still in use in 1940. Heavy and cumbersome, it was nevertheless quite reliable.

A common sight during the campaign: a pitiful group of refugees passes an German cavalry unit. It is possible that having been overtaken by the German advance, these people are returning to their homes or farms. The relatively brief duration of the campaign limited the damage to civilian property, and most refugees soon returned home.

Another formidable Maginot Line bunker complex. German troops did break through some of the more lightly defended areas of the line, but the heavily fortified sections remained in action until the surrender on June 25, 1940.

The memorial gate to a British World War I cemetery. At least the prolonged slaughter of the Great War was avoided in this instance as *blitzkrieg* was a war of maneuver, not attrition.

German personnel cars and armored cars pass
under the Arc de Triomphe in Paris. The vehicle
in the foreground appears to be an *Sd.Kfz 222* light
armored car. The Germans were quick to organize a
triumphant march through the main streets of Paris
before a gloating Adolf Hitler.

The destruction of civilian property was not extensive, but some towns and villages suffered severely from both aerial bombing and artillery fire.

Panzer crewmen enjoy the sights of one of the world's most beautiful cities.

APPENDIX A

Rank Comparisons

BRITISH ARMY	FRENCH ARMY	WAFFEN-SS	GERMAN ARMY
Enlisted Men			
Private	*Soldat*	*SS-Schütze*	*Schütze*
Private First Class		*SS-Oberschütze*	*Oberschütze*
Corporal	*Caporal*	*SS-Sturmmann*	*Gefreiter*
Senior Corporal	*Caporal-chef*	*SS-Rottenführer*	*Obergefreiter*
Staff Corporal		*SS-Stabsrottenführer*	*Stabsgefreiter*
Noncommissioned Officers			
Sergeant	*Sergeant*	*SS-Unterscharführer*	*Unteroffizier*
		SS-Scharführer	*Unterfeldwebel*
Staff Sergeant		*SS-Oberscharführer*	*Feldwebel*
Sergeant First Class	*Sergeant-chef*	*SS-Hauptcharführer*	*Oberfeldwebel*
Master Sergeant	*Adjudant*	*SS-Sturmscharführer*	*Hauptfeldwebel*
Sergeant Major	*Major*		*Stabsfeldwebel*
Officers			
Second Lieutenant	*Sous-Lieutenant*	*SS-Untersturmführer*	*Leutnant*
First Lieutenant	*Lieutenant*	*SS-Obersturmführer*	*Oberleutnant*
Captain	*Capitane*	*SS-Hauptsturmführer*	*Hauptman*
Major	*Commandant*	*SS-Sturmbannführer*	*Major*
Lieutenant Colonel	*Lieutenant-Colonel*	*SS-Obersturmbannführer*	*Oberstleutnant*
Colonel	*Colonel*	*SS-Standartenführer*	*Oberst*
Brigadier General	*Général d'Brigade*	*SS-Brigadeführer*	*Generalmajor*
Major General		*SS-Gruppenführer*	*Generalleutnant*
Lieutenant General	*Général d'Division*	*SS-Obergruppenführer*	*General der Fallschirmjäger, etc.*
General	*Général d'Corps d'Armee*	*SS-Oberstgruppenführer*	*Generaloberst*
General of the Army	*Général d'Armee*	*Reichsführer-SS*	*Feldmarschall*

BIBLIOGRAPHY

Angolia, John R., and Adolf Schlicht. *Uniforms and Traditions of the German Army, 1933–1945.* Vols. 1–3. San Jose, CA: R. J. Bender, 1984–92.

Bock, Fedor von. *Generalfeldmarschall Fedor von Bock: The War Diary, 1939–1945.* Atglen, PA: Schiffer, 1996.

Buchner, Alex. *The German Infantry Handbook, 1939–1945: Organization, Uniforms, Weapons, Equipment, Operations.* West Chester, PA: Schiffer, 1991.

Burdick, Charles, and Hans-Adolf Jacobsen, eds. *The Halder War Diary, 1939–1942.* Novato, CA: Presidio Press, 1988.

Chamberlain, Peter, and Hilary Doyle. *Encyclopedia of German Tanks of World War Two: A Complete Illustrated Directory of German Battle Tanks, Armored Cars, Self-Propelled Guns, and Semi-Tracked Vehicles, 1933–1945.* London: Arms and Armour Press, 1978.

Dictionnaire Historique. *Les Divisions de l'Armee de Terre allemande. Heer 1939–1945.* Bayeux, France: Editions Heimdal, 1997.

Doughty, Robert A. *The Breaking Point: Sedan and the Fall of France, 1940.* Hamden, CT: Archon Books, 1990.

Ellis, Chris, ed. *Wheeled Vehicles of the Wehrmacht.* Bedfordshire, England: Air Research Publications, 1988.

Forty, George, and John Duncan. *The Fall of France: Disaster in the West, 1939–40.* Kent, England: Guild Publishing, 1990.

Gander, Terry, and Peter Chamberlain. *Small Arms, Artillery, and Special Weapons of the Third Reich.* London: Macdonald and Jane's, 1978.

Gooch, John, ed. *Decisive Campaigns of the Second World War.* London: F. Cass, 1990.

Guderian, Heinz. *Panzer Leader.* London: M. Joseph, 1952.

Hogg, Ian V. *German Artillery of World War Two.* London: Arms and Armour Press, 1975.

Horne, Alistair. *To Lose a Battle: France, 1940.* London: Macmillan, 1969.

Kemp, Anthony. *The Maginot Line: Myth and Reality.* New York: Stein and Day, 1982.

Liddell Hart, Basil H. *The Other Side of the Hill: Germany's Generals, Their Rise and Fall, with Their Own Account of Military Events, 1939–1945.* London: Cassell, 1973.

Liddell Hart, Basil H., ed. *The Rommel Papers.* London: Collins, 1953.

Luck, Hans von. *Panzer Commander: The Memoirs of Colonel Hans von Luck.* New York: Praeger, 1989.

Mellenthin, F. W. von. *Panzer Battles: A Study of the Employment of Armor in the Second World War.* Norman, OK: University of Oklahoma Press, 1956.

Murray, Williamson. *Strategy for Defeat: The Luftwaffe, 1933–1945.* Maxwell AFB, AL: Air University Press, 1983.

Niehorster, Leo W. G. *German World War II Organizational Series.* Vol. 2/I. *Mechanized Army Divisions (10 May 1940).* Dunstable, England: Military Press, 2005.

———. *German World War II Organizational Series.* Vol. 2/II. *Higher Headquarters and Mechanized GHQ Units (10 May 1940).* Dunstable, England: Military Press, 2005.

Perrett, Brian. *A History of Blitzkrieg.* New York: Stein and Day, 1983.

Research Institute for Military History. *Germany and the Second World War.* Vol. 2. *Germany's Initial Conquests in Europe.* Oxford, England: Oxford University Press, 1991.

Rothbrust, Florian K. *Guderian's XIXth Panzer Corps and the Battle of France: Breakthrough in the Ardennes, May 1940.* New York: Praeger, 1990.

Senger und Etterlin, Frido von. *Neither Fear nor Hope: The Wartime Career of General Frido von Senger und Etterlin, Defender of Cassino.* Novato, CA: Presidio, 1989.

Smith, J. Richard, and Antony L. Kay. *German Aircraft of the Second World War.* London: Putnam, 1972.

Stahlberg, Alexander. *Bounden Duty: The Memoirs of a German Officer, 1932–45.* London: Brassey's, 1990.

Trevor-Roper, Hugh R., ed. *Hitler's War Directives, 1939–1945.* London: Pan, 1966.

U.S. War Department. *Handbook on German Military Forces.* Baton Rouge, LA: Louisiana State University Pres, 1990.

Warlimont, Walter. *Inside Hitler's Headquarters, 1939–45.* New York: Praeger, 1964.

ACKNOWLEDGMENTS

The following people deserve credit for their generous assistance in supplying period photographs taken by the combatants themselves, along with modern color images of uniforms, equipment, and weapons. In each and every case, they went above and beyond to help bring this book to life by offering their expertise and time: Pat Cassidy, Steve Cassidy, P. Whammond and Carey of Collector's Guild (www.germanmilitaria.com), Wilson History and Research Center (www.militaryheadgear.com), Jim Haley, David A. Jones, Jim Pool, Scott Pritchett, Phil Francis, and Aleks and Dmitri of Espenlaub Militaria (www.aboutww2 militaria.com and www.warrelics.eu/forum), as well as the National Archives, the Swedish Army Museum, and a few individuals who wish to remain anonymous.

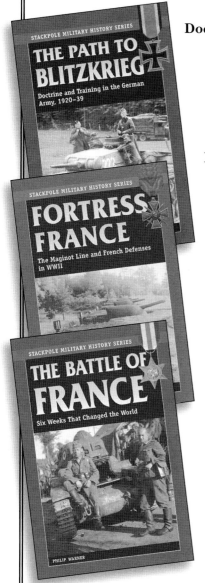
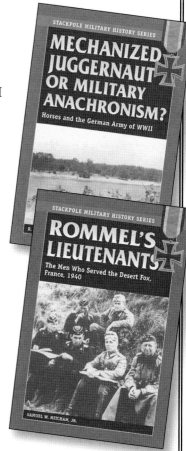